The Titan

A Business Parable with Time Travel

by
Steve Werner
www.LiveToWinCoaching.com

with
Rick Butts
www.RickButts.com

The Titan – A Business Parable with Time Travel

Disclaimer and Terms of Use: This publication is designed to provide accurate and authoritative information with regard to the subject matter covered. It is sold with the understanding that the publisher is not engaged in rendering legal, accounting, or other professional advice. If legal advice or other expert assistance is required, the services of a competent professional should be sought.

> —From a *Declaration of Principles* jointly adopted by a Committee of the American Bar Association and a Committee of Publishers and Associations.

ISBN: 1-939315-12-3

ISBN-13: 978-1-939315-12-0

Table of Contents

To The Reader

This book is short for two reasons.

1. You are busy.

2. The truth we often need to hear is not a hundred chapters long.

So, if you are feeling stuck, overwhelmed, burned out, or wondering "is that all there is?" about your business life, this book is a break-glass-in-case-of-emergency solution that will blast you through the obstacles and get you back on track at optimum speed.

Here we go!

(I told you this would be short.)

Too Late

There was no longer any use in hurrying. By the time he battled through this ferocious traffic snarl, the 9 a.m. meeting for which he was already late would be over. The fate of the business he'd poured his life into for more than a year, would be decided by two fools. Jack eased his foot from the gas pedal. The odometer floated down to five miles over the speed limit, the acceptable risk. The black SUV under his command relaxed, but slowing down his vehicle did nothing to slow down his racing thoughts.

For the last thirty minutes, he had been keeping up with the progress of the meeting via SMS messages from his assistant, who was at the conference table in their office clashing swords with the cocky attorney and the government tool who would rule on their business.

Jack glanced down to check the latest update. He never saw the traffic light turn from green to amber, or the rusty gray truck that blew through the intersection, slamming his SUV t-bone style and bulldozing him through the old cement bridge railing into the Chicago River.

Cold water filled up the SUV much faster, and louder, than it did in the movies. By the time Jack shook off the impact of the wreck and lifted his head from the steering wheel, he had only seconds to escape.

He gave the handle a pull, but the driver door would not budge, and the windows, fried by the water, would not roll down. He tore at his seat belt as the water crawled up his neck to his lips. He stretched his chin away from the water and began to understand that he was actually going to drown.

Suddenly he felt hands grabbing him hard on his arms, scraping his neck, wrenching him upward and out the window of the SUV. He kicked his legs, swimming instinctively until he broke the surface of the water. His body was being towed with his neck inside the elbow of a muscular forearm. He spat water and gasped for breath in the chop of the river.

When they arrived at the muddy bank, the man who'd brought him there laid Jack face down where he threw up the rest of the water and began breathing again.

"Well, thank God I didn't have to give you mouth-to-mouth," his rescuer said, through panting attempts to catch his own breath from the heroic swim.

"Thank you. Thank you. Thank you, man," panted Jack. "You saved my life, you know?"

"Yes, I know," the man agreed. "I nearly didn't come after you. Suicide is a sin you know?"

"Suicide? I didn't try to kill myself. Somebody hit my vehicle and I crashed into the river. You pulled me from my SUV, you know," said Jack.

"Mister, I don't know what the heck an ESS YOU BEE is, but nobody hit you. I watched you drive right off that bridge up there, and I pulled my truck over and jumped in after you." The man pointed upward and Jack's eyes followed his finger toward the sky.

What he saw made his jaw drop open with amazement. The concrete shape of the bridge looked the same, but everything else was different. Gone were the chrome and glass skyscrapers of the Chicago skyline. They were replaced by a Chicago he'd only seen before in black and white photographs.

"It looks like the 1930s," said Jack, shaking his head and rubbing his eyes.

"It's 1947," said the man.

1947

The unfamiliar squawk of cartoon-sounding horns filled the air as antique vehicles pushed and crowded along the bridge overhead. Jack stood up in his soggy loafers and did a quick 360-degree look around him. Was he dreaming? Dead?

"Are you okay, buddy?" asked the man.

"Well, I think I'm okay, except that when I went into the river it was 2013," he replied.

"2013? You using military time? No it's not that late. It's just about 9:30 in the morning."

"I mean the year 2013. I live like, what, like sixty-six years in the future from here," said the businessman, adding math to his confusion.

"Oh, great! You're not only suicidal but you're crazy," said the man. He took a long look at Jack for clues.

"I'm not crazy," said Jack. "I'm under a lot of stress, but I'm not crazy. Either I'm dreaming, or I've traveled back in time to 1947."

As the man eyed him suspiciously, Jack tried to mesh the impossibility of the words he had just spoken with the overwhelming evidence around him. "Maybe I'm asleep, or unconscious?" he thought.

He tried to wake up. He pinched his hand. He jumped up and down to get his blood flowing. And finally, he slapped himself. The world around him remained intact, including the man who'd rescued him who was staring at his antics.

A crowd of people had begun to fill the bridge and traffic had stopped at the point where his SUV had gone over. The truck the man had abandoned in order to save him was sitting with the door open, blocking one lane. Sirens could be heard in the distance, getting closer.

A policeman half walked, half slid down the embankment to where they were standing and demanded to know what happened. The man told his story. Jack discovered that his name was Theodore Whitman—"Ted"—as he told how he had rescued the stranger just moments before. He was a truck driver who just happened to see the accident and stepped in to help. And, yes, that was his truck blocking all the traffic up on the bridge.

"What about you Mister, what's your name?" said the policeman.

"Jack," said Jack.

"And what's your address?"

Jack opened his mouth to give his address and then realized that if he truly was in 1947 his address probably didn't even exist. He visibly frowned and looked at Ted. Ted shook his head no as if he understood Jack's dilemma.

"I'm in town on business. I'm staying at The Palmer House," he said.

Jack had lived in Chicago his whole life. He yanked the name of a famous old hotel out of his emergency memory from school. Everyone knew about The Palmer House. It seemed to be enough for the cop for now.

"Okay, buddy, you were a good guy to help this fella out of the river, but you need to go move your truck along now. Let's get out of here." said the policeman, closing his report book and turning to go up the embankment.

"Hey! What about my, uh, car?" asked Jack.

"What about it?" said the cop.

"Won't the city pull it out of the river?"

"Buddy, your car is gone. The city's not going to come down here and spend a lot of money fishing it out of this river. What for? It's just a hunk of metal now. Let's go." The policeman and Ted headed up to the street, leaving Jack standing all alone by the river. He looked at the water. He looked at the gothic spires of the old-style Chicago buildings. He looked at the men disappearing up the hill and reluctantly followed.

The Truck

"Mister, I have places to go and things to do," said Ted, checking the boxes strapped in the bed of his truck. "You can come with me, and I'll drop you off wherever you want to go along the way," he said.

The policeman seemed okay with that, and motioned for Ted to get his truck moving. He had plenty to do now clearing the massive traffic jam, and then he'd have to complete yet another report.

Ted's truck was at the front of the traffic mess and there was nothing but wide open, clear pavement ahead. He was back on the road quickly. He watched his passenger stare in open amazement at the world around him. If a man were to get into a car crash and wake up sixty-six years in the past, how would he act? Ted guessed he would probably act just the way Jack was.

"I've lived in Chicago my whole life," said Jack. "I love the history of this city. I've seen photographs of this era but only in black and white. To see this place alive and vibrant and in living color is just incredible."

"Living color?" asked Ted.

"Oh," laughed Jack, "that will be a marketing description in the future of the new color film technology they'll use in motion pictures. 'In glorious, living color!'"

"You mentioned marketing," said Ted. "Not a lot of people around here know what that word means."

"Really?" said Jack, "In the future, marketing will become the single most critical factor in the success or failure of your business. Over time the process of creating a good product, controlling costs, and setting up a business that works will be pretty much simple. The winners and losers will be determined by who can most effectively get customers to consider their offering."

"What about inventing new products, new tools, new processes?" asked Ted.

"That's the surest way to really hit it big in business now."

"Well, you said it's 1947 right now?" asked Jack.

"Yes."

"In about twelve years, America will begin manned space flight in orbit around the planet, and in exactly twenty-two years we will send a team of men to the moon along with a vehicle to drive around on it, collect samples, and come back," said Jack.

"You're kidding me?" said Ted. Space flight? To the moon? It seemed outrageous but in his own lifetime he'd seen the airplane invented, and when Charles Lindbergh flew the Lindy from New York to England, many people thought that was impossible.

"Listen, you don't look like someone from the future. For one thing, why are you wearing normal clothes?" Ted inspected Jack's apparel. "Shouldn't you have on some special outfit from the future?"

Jack looked down and realized he was not wearing the khaki slacks, button down dress shirt, and black penny loafers he went into the water wearing but instead was wearing a wool pinstripe suit. It was still damp to the touch but a pretty nice suit.

His fingers traced the fabric and tugged on one suspender.

"You do have a strange haircut," Ted continued. "And you don't really talk like anyone I've ever met in Chicago." He paused to think. "So, let's say you are from the future. How did you get here? Why are you here? What are you gonna do?"

"I'm not sure why I'm here," said Jack. "I mean, I didn't plan this. I was just driving along and got in an accident, and now I'm here. I'm not even sure if you and this whole thing are just a dream."

"Well, I'm not dreaming," said Ted. "I've got work to do, and places to go."

"What else can I do now—tap my heels together three times and say, 'There's no place like home, Toto'?"

"Tap your heels and what?" asked Ted.

"That's from a movie called the Wizard of Oz." Jack paused. Was the Wizard of Oz even out in 1947?

"I've heard about it," said Ted. "First part is in black and white and then goes into color. I've not seen it."

"Well, Toto, we're not in Kansas anymore."

"Of course not," said Ted, rolling his eyes. "This is Illinois. If you don't have anywhere to go then you can ride along with me and help me deliver these boxes."

Ted jerked his thumb toward the rear window where stacks of boxes and small crates sat in the bed of the truck. "Maybe your head will clear and you'll figure out which mental hospital you escaped from, or something will look familiar to you as we go."

"Ok," said Jack. With no real alternative coming to mind, riding along in Ted's truck seemed a lot better than walking nowhere alone.

"Do you like coffee and donuts?" asked Ted.

"Well, of course. Everyone likes donuts. But I'm really careful about carbs and getting too much sugar, or I'll have to spend a lot of extra time in the gym," said Jack.

"Carbs? Watching sugar? In the gym? What are you now, a boxer?" asked Ted.

"What do you mean, 'boxer'?" Jack replied.

"Well, who else spends time in a gym?" said Ted.

But Jack was no longer listening. He was looking around at a sight no one in his generation had ever seen. Chicago in 1947 was vivid, noisy, bustling—and everything was an amazing antique-come-to-life reality show.

The truck pulled up along a busy street and parked in front of Flo's Delicious Donuts. "Here we are. Best donuts and coffee on earth. Get your taste buds ready."

Ted set the parking brake and leapt out of the cab of the truck.

Donuts and Coffee

Before Jack walked through the open door of Flo's Coffee Shop, the smell of warm fresh donuts swept over him, and he was instantly hungry.

"Put those right over here on the counter, Ted," said a slender blonde woman behind the counter wearing a blue waitress uniform, apron, and surprisingly, a tan baseball cap. Wiping her hands on a towel, she removed the lid off the top box, pulled out a sheet of thick paper, and surveyed the page. "Ted, you've done it again! These are great!"

"Hey, all I do is put your ideas on paper, Flo, and I think you have some really good ideas," said Ted.

"Right you are!" said Flo. "You boys want some coffee?" she asked, surveying Jack and talking to Ted. "I've got some new stuff in from Columbia, and we just glazed a new batch of donuts."

"Wow! I don't eat donuts much, you know, carbs and sugar and all," said Jack, patting his flat stomach.

"Yeah, right," said Flo as she placed two cups in saucers on the counter and motioned for them to sit down on the barstools. A dark-haired woman came through the swinging doors with a large plate of donuts along with two small plates which she placed in front of them.

"Thanks Blanche," said Ted, smiling at her and popping a donut in his mouth. "Oh my! These are little bits of heaven!"

"Who's your sidekick here?" asked Flo.

"This is Jack," said Ted.

"Good to meet ya, Jack." Flo shook his hand, surprising him at the strength in her grip. It must have shown on his face because she smiled and said, "I worked in an airplane factory during the war. Got some muscles now."

"A regular Rosie the Riveter!" laughed Jack, referring to the World War II poster depicting a plucky homemaker turned factory worker for the war effort.

"Yes, we can!" said Flo, smiling and striking the pose from the "We Can Do It" poster, empowering the American working woman's can-do attitude that filled manufacturing and other jobs while the men were fighting overseas.

"Jack, what are you doing riding around with this character?" She nodded Ted's way.

"Well, I..." Jack wasn't sure what to say. He surely couldn't just blurt out his time travel paradigm. What was he doing here?

"Yes, you can tell that Jack is not my delivery boy," said Ted. "Jack's a business man, like yourself ...uh, business woman. Well, you know what I mean."

"What kind of business are you in then, Jackie boy?" asked Flo.

"I'm involved with several businesses, several very different businesses, in fact. Some of them I've bought in progress, and some of them I started from scratch, just like you are doing here, Flo." said Jack.

"Very impressive." said Flo.

"Well, thanks, Flo." said Jack, taking another donut bite and sip of coffee. "I've got a big decision to make about what's next for me, though."

"Well, if you need to make a decision about your business my friend, you're sure spending time with the right guy. You obviously know Ted's story then?" asked

"Flo", Ted gave her a look that told her not to continue.

"No. Actually we just met very recently," said Jack. "I was in a car accident, and Ted picked me up—rescued me actually—and now we're riding around in his truck. It's all happened kind of fast. I don't even know what we're delivering."

"Printing!" said Flo. "Teddy boy sold his… well, he started this printing business and he's darn good at it." She pulled a sample from the box and handed it to Ted.

The Amazing Story of Coffee was the headline on the top of the paper, with a drawing of a man wearing a wide hat standing next to a burro with large open bags on each side filled with what he assumed must be coffee beans.

"Juan Valdez?" asked Jack, surveying the rest of the advertisement.

Ted and Flo gave him a puzzled look.

"Never mind," said Jack as he continued reading.

Deep in the high altitude jungles of Columbia the coffee you are drinking right now started it's life…. The story was quite interesting and the copy was written in that special, confident, positive attitude that described much of the business philosophy and advertising of post-World War II America.

The story of coffee turned into the story of how Flo discovered the different kinds of coffee from around the world—from friends returning from war and travel overseas—and how she began her quest to bring something special to Chicago.

Flo's Coffee N' Donuts and her address sat in bold font at the bottom along with a coupon for a free donut with a cup of coffee to new visitors to the store.

"This is pretty cool," said Jack.

"You've got to know your story," said Flo. "Ted taught me that."

"What do you mean?" asked Jack.

"When you are making choices about your life, what direction to pursue, where to put your time and energy, all of that, it's essential that you know your story, where you came from, what shaped you, in order to know where to go. Right?" asked Flo.

"Well, I never really thought of it like that but, sure," said Jack.

"It's no different in business, because as an entrepreneur you really LIVE your business. So, in order to make decisions that keep you in alignment with your core values and beliefs, I believe you have to know your story," said Flo. For instance, what kind of decision do you need to make about your business?"

"I'm in a bit of a dilemma about a new opportunity that has come my way," said Jack. It felt funny to tell someone else what had been bouncing around in his head. In fact he wasn't sure he had told anyone what was going on inside him lately.

"Right now I've got a fairly complex situation that's breathing down my neck with a new business I took over," he said, "but that's not what keeps me awake at night. This dilemma about choosing my future path, as you said, is what's most troubling to me."

Jack took a sip of his coffee and finished the donut on his plate. These were amazing donuts and, to his gourmet palate, the coffee was remarkably better than he had expected in a little diner in 1947.

"Well, you're with friends," Ted smiled. "Tell us about this big dilemma."

Jack thought for a moment, then began slowly. "All of my businesses are special to me in their own way, and quite different."

"Like children?" asked Ted.

"Yes, quite a lot like that," Jack agreed. "I have three great kids, but they are all very different, and I love them for their gifts and for the challenges they bring me as a father."

"Good. But five sounds like a lot to keep track of," said Flo.

"It can get complicated, but I'm a part of a great partnership, with entrepreneurs like me, and managers who do a good job of handling many of the details so I can concentrate on the things I'm good at—and on my favorite thing, people and the big picture. I've built them from scratch or got them when they were small, so I was very involved in how they work. So I feel pretty good about not being frontline all the time."

"Like children," said Flo.

"Like children." Jack smiled thinking about the people in each business and about the early days, the infancy, when he put in crazy long hours trying to get them to sustainable profitability. "Now they're grown up and I'm not sure what's next for them... or for me."

"How do you mean?" asked Ted.

"Well, I'm kind of at the point where I feel like what I ought to do is to choose just one, put all my energy into it, and bring my focus and creativity into building a much bigger company than any of these will ever be now," said Jack.

"That sounds like a great idea, a worthy challenge," said Ted. "What would happen to the other kids?"

"I guess I'd put them up for sale or figure out some type of buyout with the existing management. Finance is my background and I'm pretty good at figuring out that sort of thing," said Jack.

"Actually, I'm not so worried about how to find a home for any of these businesses or, for that matter, all of them. And that's what I've been thinking about doing lately.

"If you sell them all, what will you do? Retire?" asked Ted.

Jack sipped his coffee. He had never told anyone what he had been thinking about, and he had thought about it a lot lately. Maybe it would be easier to tell a stranger. "I've been thinking a lot lately about getting completely out of the management business, and doing a one-man operation," said Jack.

"Sounds good to me," said Ted. "That's exactly what I've done." He pointed at the box of freshly printed pages sitting on the counter.

"Wow. Ok. Good for you Ted." Jack smiled. "But if I tell my employees, my partners, heck, even my wife that I want to do this," he paused, "there's going to be a lot of blowback. I simply do not know what to do."

"Well, I know exactly what you should do," announced Flo. "You should have another donut and coffee!" She laughed, and they all agreed. Flo disappeared through the swinging doors into the bakery.

Know Your Story

Ted and Jack returned to the truck and by noon began driving to the next delivery.

"I think Flo is right on this one, Jack. It would be helpful for you to make a decision about the future by looking at the path you took to get here. When you think back on your choices in business and life, what stands out to you?" asked Ted.

Jack thought for a moment, and then smiled. "When I was in the sixth grade I got the bright idea to write to the oil companies who sponsored race cars and try to get them to send me the promotional decals they used. You know, with their logo on them," said Jack. "At first I got no response, but I didn't give up. I got better at writing the letters. I literally begged them and bothered them until they would send me an entire manila envelope stuffed with stickers!"

"I took these stickers to school and around my neighborhood and sold them, then took the money I made from the stickers and played poker with it. That year I parlayed $5 into $500! I realize $500 is not a lot of money, but I was the richest kid in the sixth grade, and I was the guy with the stickers, too."

"That's a great story, Jack," said Ted. "And I think it's important. It says a lot about your nature and instincts to have done that at such an early age. What else?"

"Well, my great uncles and my father all worked at Maxwell Street, this huge bazaar or flea market where peddlers of all sorts sold their goods."

"I'm very familiar with Maxwell Street," said Ted, "in fact, we're going there today."

"Really?" said Jack. "That's fantastic! I wonder if I could meet one of my relatives there."

"Time travel again?" asked Ted.

"Yes. Okay, listen. My dad wore wrist watches as he still refers to them, up and down his arms under a long trench coat. He began peddling at the age of ten to help subsidize his family's income. He always had a wad of bills in his pocket from his direct sales business.

"So in 1979 I'm in college at Arizona State. My roommate and I stumble upon this gigantic flea market that ran on Saturday and Sunday mornings and afternoons at the Greyhound race track. I begin to notice that people are selling everything. Clothes, watches, rings, shoes, you name it. I sense an opportunity, and tell my roommate that I have an idea. We go back to our house to discuss my idea. I tell him I know of a discount wholesale company in Chicago that sells jewelry and electronics, and I tell him a little of my family history doing business on Maxwell Street. I tell him how we can make some serious money."

"A-ha, wholesale, retail," laughed Ted. "So, how do you buy your first inventory?"

"My plan is to have my father send us a catalogue from this wholesale store. We order inventory, my dad air ships it to us and we hustle the products, mostly watches and rings, at the flea market."

"We go to Greyhound Park the next Saturday at 4 a.m. to explore the process. It turns out that they sell you one parking spot for $10, and some big vendors have as many as ten to twenty spots set up. I begin to have a vision. We pool all of our money together, like $100, and purchase inventory. We get watches for $5 to $7 and rings at $3 to $4. I call my dad and go over the order, and he air freights to Sky Harbor Airport. We drive and pick up the goods. Come Saturday morning we get to Grey Hound Park at 3 a.m. The earlier you arrive the better chance you have to pick the spot you want. Location is everything. We buy our $10 spot and lay out our inventory on the hood of my 1977 white Trans Am. We're in business."

"What's a Trans Am?" asked Ted.

"Oh, it's a car—a rather fancy sports car," said Jack. "Soon Detroit will start a marketing campaign that focuses on the changes made to each year's model of their cars, and emphasize the importance of "new" versus "used" cars to get people to buy new ones. That's why I mention the year my car was made, 1977."

"1977..." Ted gazed ahead as he navigated the delivery truck around a large pothole in the street. "When we have the time you'll have to tell me what the future holds for us. Ok?"

"Yes," said Jack, realizing he had no idea from one moment to the next if he was staying in this era—or how to get home. "Of course. Much has happened."

"Okay, tell me the rest of your story," Ted said.

"Okay. We spend all day hustling our merchandise. Of course the temperature in Phoenix is 107, and the inventory is heating up on the metal of the car like it's on a grill. But, this does not stop us. At the end of the day we count up our profits, and we've made about $150 after selling out," Jack said.

"Were you excited?" asked Ted.

"Oh my gosh, yes. Over the coming weeks we begin to expand, eventually purchasing a collapsible tent, table, and glass show cases. We grow from one parking spot to four spots very quickly.

"We create a system and we use the same procedure every week. We reinvest our profits to buy more inventory and business necessities. We order through my dad every week on Tuesday and pick up the goods on Thursday. Eventually, we grow the business to where we're making a few hundred dollars apiece. Pretty good for college students in the late 70s early 80s." Jack paused.

"When we graduated, we sold the tent, tables, and showcases at a slight markup to a fellow named Nick the Greek, who was also hustling at the same venue. But we were entrepreneurs!"

"Bravo!" said Ted. "I love a great business startup story!"

17

"Thanks, Ted. You're kind to listen." Jack replied. "But, look—do these stories tell me what I should do with my business, and my life, going forward?"

"When you think about your path into the future, I think it's vital that you know your story, and what it says about you, the lessons you've learned and the values your story have ingrained in you," said Ted. "Think on these things. Write them down and what they mean to you. Then point these lessons into your future and let what you do know illuminate your path forward."

Jack listened to Ted intently, deep in thought.

"Here." Ted pulled a small leather book out of a box behind his seat. With one hand on the wheel he fanned the pages toward Jack with his thumb.

"A book?" asked Jack.

"No. Better," said Ted. "It's a journal. I made a few of these for one of my customers. The pages are all blank. If you write down the problems you are trying to solve, the ones that you feel most conflicted about, and then what you've learned about your story as it applies to this matter, you will begin to see your answer in front of you."

Jack took the journal. The leather felt good in his hands. As they drove deeper into the city, Jack began making some notes in the journal.

Never Be Satisfied

As a long dream starts to feel real, you adapt. You talk to the people in your dream and take actions and make choices in the dream world, even if you know it doesn't make sense. For only in real life do you feel comfortable shouting, "I must be dreaming!".

Jack spent the afternoon in such a world. Knowing full well he was not in 1947 Chicago—that would be impossible—but lacking an explanation for the sights, sounds, and people around him, he went with it. The experience was amazing.

At each stop along the way Ted introduced him to another interesting entrepreneur who had purchased printing from this unusual man. Each one in turn had something important to say; at least it seemed so to Jack, bringing increasing clarity to the confusion of his business, and his life.

There was the fish market down by the lake where he met an energetic Asian couple who had come to the US as war refugees and, despite prejudice and no resources, had started a small market and grown it with hustle and pride.

Customers lined up and waited their turn, each receiving special attention, a good deal, and a laugh.

Sitting in a small back room for a cup of tea, they examined the flyer they had created with the same enthusiasm they showed their best customers. Jack listened to their story of surviving the war, the harrowing journey to the strange machineworld of the US from a village without a single motor car, and how they slept on burlap bags at the back of the market when they started their business. But far from complaining about life, fate, or business, they were infinitely enthusiastic about the future.

When Jack asked the wife what she believed was the secret to their business success, she looked at her husband with a smile and said, "My husband say never be satisfied. He say always look for better way, better system, better result. He say when you always look for better, life always get better."

She adjusted her husband's collar and brushed some stray debris from his shirt, obviously very much in love with the smiling man, and proud. "I want to kill him many times," she laughed, "but he turns out to be right about better."

"When you always look for better, no matter when things go wrong, eventually most things improve," agreed the husband. "Never be satisfied. Always look for better. That's the thing!"

The sun had started to dip in the western sky, and the shadows drew long as they headed to what Ted said was the last stop. The bed of the truck was empty except for one small box that Ted had roped in tightly near the cab and covered with an army green tarp to protect it from the light rain that had begun to fall.

"Where are we going now?" asked Jack with a smile of anticipation.

"You mentioned Maxwell Street earlier, right?" asked Ted.

"Yes, I did," said Jack. "My great uncle used to run a street vendor business down there after World War II."

"Jack, it is after World War II right now."

Draw the Line

Maxwell Street was known at the largest open air market in the country in its day and, if today was any example, that rumor had to be true. The moment Ted turned the corner the whole scene exploded in a chaos of commerce.

A sea people of people from all ethnicities and, apparently, all income levels spilled off the sidewalks and into the streets moving like crowds down the midway at a carnival. Stores were crammed together with windows full of merchandise and their doors open, often accompanied by a street display in the front where shopkeepers or employees hawked and haggled over their wares.

"This is crazy!" said Jack. They had driven around Chicago most of the day but had seen nothing that even came close to comparing to this.

"Yeah, there are businesses down here that have been here for years and others that popped up last night. There are so many customers down here it's a real temptation for the entrepreneurial person to scratch their small business itch and setup shop here," said Ted.

The sound of drums, bass, harmonica, guitar and then singing rose above the crowd noise and got louder as they continued down the street. A small group of blues musicians was jamming hard on the sidewalk in front of a saloon. They were surrounded by people dancing and shouting, pouring in to the saloon for refreshments and out of the saloon to shop with a buzz.

"Maxwell Street attracts a lot of poor people in need of jobs and people looking for a big discount on everything from clothes, appliances, cars, and tools to just about anything anyone might want," Ted continued. "Some of the merchandise down here is hijacked or stolen from delivery trucks or pirated from railroad cars, but it's nearly impossible for the police to stop. If the price is right, happy customers don't ask a lot of questions."

The crowd magically parted as Ted guided the truck to the side and parked snuggly up against the curb in front of a pawn shop. He removed the small tarp and untied the last box in the back. Jack followed him into the pawn shop.

"Ted!" shouted a voice from behind the counter, "Mazaltav, my friend!"

"Ben, so good to see you," answered Ted. "I've got your order right here."

"Excellent. Let's have a look," said Ben.

Ted placed the box on the counter, whipped out a small pocketknife and cut the tape that held the box tight. He pried open the flaps and lifted out one of several small, white, rectangular boxes and handed it to Ben.

"Oh, my goodness! These are just what I had in mind," said Ben as he flipped the top off the smaller white box and lifted out one crisp business card. He rubbed the parchment stock between his thumb and forefinger and nodded his head approvingly. "Perfect."

"May I see?" asked Jack.

Ben looked over at Jack, and Ted realized he'd failed to introduce the stranger he'd brought in with him.

"Oh, sorry. Ben, this is Jack," he said. "Jack is riding with me today and helping me out. Jack, meet my good friend and serial entrepreneur Ben."

The two men shook hands and Ben handed Jack the business card. "Very nice, but why doesn't it say 'pawn shop'?" asked Jack.

"That's a very good question," said Ben. "Should I tell him, Ted?

Ted nodded his approval.

"You see, this pawn shop here is sort of a base of operations for my family business. A pawn shop—especially a pawn shop on Maxwell Street—is a very interconnected operation. We loan money on all sorts of items, but people use the money for a whole lot of reasons that aren't necessarily to make ends meet or to stretch to payday."

"People borrow money from us to start a business, buy a sign, rent a cart, and purchase inventory to bring here to sell. Everything is in motion down here all the time. But what people don't always see is the other side of our business—we are a regular store.

"We may acquire our inventory in an unusual way, by buying it from individuals. We also supplement our inventory by purchasing some of it elsewhere. We're in the money business, and we are right in the middle of a whole world of deals. So, in order to take advantage of other opportunities, we go out into the suit-and-tie side of Chicago and do business with a whole other group of people who would never set foot in a pawn shop."

"So, that's why you need a great looking business card, right?" asked Jack.

"Yes, exactly," said Ben, "we run many businesses, and this card is really an umbrella for all our ambitions."

"It's complicated, isn't it?" asked Jack. "I run multiple businesses myself. There are a lot of people and numbers to keep track of, aren't there?"

"You can say that again. We used to have one crisis after another because no one could remember a particular deal that one of us had made, and around here," Ben waved his hand palms up around the cases and shelves of every sort of product imaginable, "it is very easy for anything to get lost."

"Well, you sure don't look disorganized now," said Jack. "The place looks clean and neat, and everyone around here seems to move about the store with purpose, like they know what to do so they don't waste time when you're busy."

"Well, thank you, Jack," said Ben, smiling at the compliment. "You have a very good eye for detail, my friend. Actually, it was Ted here who helped us to set up systems—systems for taking in merchandise, for loans, for selling inventory. Heck, once we started setting up systems and writing down procedures, it really started to snowball around here."

"I came in here one day and Ben had actually drawn up a system for getting lunch, for crying out loud!" laughed Ted.

"Hey, you can laugh if you want but the system worked. We still use it today. We just find that when people know what to do, things get done, and they get done faster and with fewer problems, and our employees ask us a heck of a lot fewer questions, too," said Ben. "The less time I spend answering questions or making the same decision over and over, the more time I have to do more important things only I can do, and more time for my personal and family life."

"There is no question that you're right," said Jack. "We have a saying in my business: any problem that happens more than two times… design a solution, make it into a system, and teach it to everyone. So we say, 'when this happens, here's what we do.' And we don't freak out and try to call the boss!"

"It's a waste of time to reinvent the wheel every day, and we get much happier customers because they don't have to see the look on the face of an employee who doesn't know what to do in handling a problem they're having," said Ben.

Ben invited the men to take a tour of the store and showed them some of his systems, setup with painted lines for box stacking, and charts and printed instructions as well as some posters with steps on them for what to do in different situations. The lunch system was a large piece of cardboard taped to the refrigerator in the back room where they ate lunch and held meetings.

They walked through the warehouse, and Jack marveled at the amount of inventory this small pawn shop held—far from the eyes of the average visitor in from the street. Ben explained that they were known to be a great resource for purchasing agents at growing companies in the Chicago area. Because Ben bought truckloads of seconds, returned orders, freight-damaged loads, and the like, he often got calls for everything from dozens of uniforms to tools, motors, women's lingerie, and baby bottles.

"The items in this warehouse would be worth millions in this condition in my time," Jack whispered to Ted. "The furniture, the machines, the clothing, and bicycles… everything in here is treasure to my age."

"What do you mean?" asked Ted, looking around the warehouse. "I thought you had space ships and all this modern technology? Who would pay anything for this old junk in the future?"

"Antiques, Ted. People in my world are fascinated with the past, and they pay a lot of money for collectibles," said Jack.

"That seems crazy," said Ted. "Who wouldn't want the latest and greatest of everything?"

Finally they had toured the entire facility and had walked through dozens of doors that went in and out of small houses sitting next to the main store. Ben explained that they had bought these properties as he developed all the area around the shop.

It was a packrat's paradise. Ben claimed he and his brothers knew where everything was and could get it in ten seconds.

The men settled in around the table just behind the big mirror that hung behind the main sales area, a large saloon bar from the 1800s. It was carved with ornate figures of dance hall girls, cowboys, and animals.

"Wow! You can see everything that's going on in the store from here. What a terrific idea to put in a one-way mirror that reflects light to the store customers, but lets you see right into the store," said Jack.

The conversation flowed among the business people. Eventually they came to the subject of Jack's decision.

Ben turned to Jack. "So, Jack, can you tell me a little bit about your big decision? I'm interested in what other business people are working on."

"Ok, sure, I guess so...," said Jack, taking out the journal he'd been writing in. He placed it flat on the table and drew five circles. "I've got five businesses now and each one of them is operating at above average cash flow. I'm happy about this. They all have their challenges, but for the most part they are through the adolescent stage and growing nicely."

"But...?" asked Ted "I hear a big 'but' coming here soon."

"The problem is not with the businesses, it's with me," said Jack, drawing a stick figure in the center of the five circles. "I'm just not that interested in babysitting them, running them day to day. It feels too safe. There's no challenge. I worked so hard to get to this point, but I never thought about what it would be like after I got here."

"Are you bored?" asked Ben.

"Well, I'm way too busy to be bored," Jack replied. "I've got plenty to do and, believe me, I am grateful for the success. But I don't feel challenged by the routine."

"Well, why not just sell them all and go do something else?" Ted asked.

"I've thought about that, but I also thought maybe what I should do is sell… or convince one of my partners to buy me out and concentrate on taking one of them as far as I possibly can," said Jack. "Kind of like the old days, just putting all my energy and creativity into seeing how big I could grow it."

"What an interesting idea!" Ben leaned back in his chair and looked out across his store through the mirror. "I don't know… that sounds like an intriguing challenge. But when I think about me doing it, it doesn't sound so good."

"Why not?" asked Jack.

"Doing all these businesses, for me, is about making money, for sure. But, more than that, it's about all the people I get to interact with. I love being an influence here on Maxwell Street, helping people, and making things work," said Ben.

"Taking just one of them and trying to squeeze maximum success out of it is a worthy goal, to be sure, but to me it sounds too much about keeping score with the money. I don't mean it would be bad for you, just for me."

"The money would be nice, and yes, that's a valid measurement of business success, right gentlemen?" asked Jack. The others nodded and smiled.

"Is that your only decision? Is that your only option? To hold your cards and run these companies, or to focus on taking one as far as you can?" asked Ted.

"Well, honestly guys, there is something else." Jack leaned in to the table and drew a sixth circle away from the others, a much bigger circle. The other men leaned in to look as he continued. "For the longest time I've been wanting to coach other business people, to teach them what I've learned, to help them solve problems, and to handle transitions in their business lives."

"Very interesting, Jack." Ted nodded his approval. "Does that sound good to you?"

"Oh brother, does it!" said Jack, rising taller in his chair, obviously excited. "I love using my experience to figure out new challenges and to work on businesses with other owners. Everywhere I go, I'm always looking at how people 'do business,' just like looking at your operation here. It just gets me so excited, and the people I've been helping so far say they really like having someone who understands what it's like at this level, instead of their spouse, vendors, or employees."

"Why don't you do it, then?" asked Ben. "Put those other businesses up for sale—or get one of your qualified people to run them—and go for what you really want to do!"

Jack slumped forward and sat quietly in his chair. Was it really that easy?

Finally, Ben spoke. "Most people I speak with settle for less than they ever really wanted out of life …less in terms of their income, relationships, and almost anything that requires time and energy.

"I have several friends and potential clients who tell me they just want to get by. They just want to make a living, they just want to survive. They simply don't expect as much out of life as they used to. They seem to be worn down and tired."

"Stuck, like me," said Jack.

"Times have changed… things are changing fast now that the war is over. We've gotten older, and economic conditions are tougher." Ted looked right at Jack. "But one thing has not changed—you get out what you put in!"

"I know what you mean," said Jack. "I have many friends who say, 'I just need to make this much money per month to survive.' These are the same warriors who, years ago, may have made $10,000 a day in their careers. People with seven-figure incomes in the past, now just want to get by? Seriously?"

"I just can't comprehend it," Ted continued. "The world is full of abundance. There is so much out there for the taking!

"Don't get me wrong. What people are willing to 'settle' for is still a lot of money. Much more than the average person makes in a year. But why would anyone ever want to settle for 'anything'? Why not get the most out of life and what it has to offer?

"The answer seems to be that people are worn down, many times by circumstances that are beyond their control. But many times the circumstances were in their control, like business, relationship, or even health related issues."

"I get what you're saying," said Jack. "I can get really excited about striking out on my own in the coaching, consulting, speaking, and writing direction, but I'm really going to shake up a lot of people. And how do I explain this to my wife, my family? I just can't see how to get from here to there."

"Jack, here is a recipe for getting restarted, if you are up for the challenge. It's simple. I call it Drawing The Line," said Ted, taking Jack's journal and sliding it to his side of the table. "Remember, we always tend to focus on the bad and to look first at the not-so-good things that are going on in our lives. So, be prepared to accept the fact that there are positive things working in your life. Now let's begin."

Ted took Jack's journal, turned the page, and drew a vertical line down the middle between the two open facing pages.

"On the left side, write down everything that is currently working in your life. Be sure to be honest with yourself! There is a lot more good going on than you ever realized. Because these items seem to be in control, make a conscious effort to maintain them along the way.

"On the right side of the paper, start writing down a list of things that are just not working in your life at the moment. Take your time and again, be honest with yourself.

"When you're done creating the not working list, I want you to rate each item individually on a scale of one to five. One means you can live with this today, four or above means this issue is unbearable and needs to be addressed immediately.

The next step is to put the threes and below on the back burner for now. You'll be back to those soon enough.

"Now look at the issues you described as most critical, the fours and the fives, the issues that are causing the most stress in your life. Think to yourself, 'What can I do in the next sixty to ninety days to make a small impact on any of these issues? What actions can I take to get myself moving in a positive direction that will allow me to start to create some relief in these particular areas of my life?'"

Jack looked down at what Ted had written in his journal. He began to imagine what to write on each side of The Line. Already the clouds in his mind were beginning to part.

"It's really that easy, isn't it?" he asked.

"Actually, in your situation, you need to begin by giving yourself permission to do what you want. To say that it's not possible means that we are not free, we are not self-directed. We are under the control of others and have no choices. I know you don't believe that, do you, Jack?" said Ted, tossing the pen on the journal as a challenge.

"Wow!" said Jack, "I never thought of it like that. I spend so much time thinking about tactics, and putting out fires. I guess I never did actually just imagine I could just decide to do this and then let the solutions follow."

Ted continued. "Once you start to look at your life and business issues in small pieces as opposed to these massive total entities, it will allow you to move forward. As you start to move forward, look back on these worksheets to evaluate the progress you've made and start attacking the less stressful items on your list…that is, if they're even still there at all."

Ben had been silent for some time. Watching Ted work with Jack was fascinating to him. He finally spoke. "Jack, Ted is right about drawing the line. It's such a great way to mentally experiment with our choices. Ted showed this to me three years ago when I was just a little pawn shop owner, and I dreamed about expanding my business way out of my comfort zone."

"Well, that obviously was a good decision," said Jack, smiling.

"Yes, so it would seem now," said Ben, "but at the time it was such a crazy idea that I couldn't even tell my wife. My brother and I started out down here on The Street buying products from the docks and selling them on a street cart. She was tired of taking risks and very happy to just run the pawn shop."

"What was it that motivated you to move forward?" asked Jack.

"I can answer that," interrupted Ted. "Ben loves to help people. Of course, he loves the hustle, the deal, making the sale, and a good business deal, but if you want to see him really light up, watch what happens when he meets a young person with talent, drive, and potential."

"Uncle Ben! Hey! Hey! Hey!" A young boy burst through the door like he owned the place and ran right up to Ben shouting.

"Easy boy, what's going on?" Ben turned around to face the boy who wiped raindrops and sweat from his forehead and wiped his hand on his pants. He rolled up the sleeve of his small suit to reveal wristwatches crowded side by side all the way up his arm.

"Uncle Ben, I got this lady out front who's looking for a watch, and I don't have what she wants. You got one back here in the warehouse, and if you loan it to me, I'll go sell it to her now and bring you back the money," said the boy excitedly.

"Okay, just a minute. I'll get it for you." Ben excused himself from the table.

The boy surveyed Ted and Jack for a moment, then burst into a big smile. "Hi! My name is Will, I'm Ben's nephew. Pleased to meet ya," he said, sticking his hand out and giving a firm handshake in turn to each man.

"Good to meet you young man," said Jack.

"Mister, you don't have a watch?" he asked, noticing Jack's bare arm with a trained eye. "I can help you out with that," he said rolling his sleeve up. "What do you like… big and masculine, or small and elegant?"

Jack laughed at the miniature salesman and started to say he'd quit wearing a watch since he started using a smart phone, but he obviously couldn't say that.

"Let's see what you got there...," said Jack, leaning down to examine the young man's armful of inventory.

Give the Gift

The two men rode along silently, each with his own thoughts. Jack finally stopped writing in the journal, sat back in the seat, and let out a long deep sigh.

"Got some good notes?" asked Ted.

"The 'Know Your Story' idea really got me thinking," said Jack. "I've started to see a clear pattern emerging about what I'm really drawn to doing the most. There is one big problem that has also appeared, side by side, with every situation."

"Well, that can be a helpful observation," Ted added. "If we keep having the same problem over and over, that's kind of a clue, don't you think?"

"Yeah, in this case it's a clue to a perpetual problem for which there appears to be no real solution," said Jack.

"No solution?" said Ted. "You mean you've discovered the immovable object?"

"It's not an object for me, it's people," Jack answered. "Every time I draw the line you showed me, it runs smack dab into people who are standing right in the way."

"Tell me more," said Ted. "What kind of people problems are you talking about?"

"I've got relatives, partners, vendors, and customers, and it just seems like I have to dance around them to get things done, and that I spend a lot more of my time figuring out how to get things done in spite of them than I do actually working on the business." Jack stopped and looked down at his notes.

"Why don't you try giving me an example," said Ted.

"Have you ever had a friend or relative or business associate who's high maintenance? I mean ridiculously high maintenance?" asked Jack, looking out the window as vehicles and machines he'd only seen in old black and white photographs rolled by.

"I'm talking about the type of people who would put their own personal issues or agendas ahead of yours, but who expect you to do just the opposite. Each time you make a move in life they either feel insulted, neglected or left out."

"I think I get where you're going with this," said Ted. "I recently had lunch with a client who was describing this type of situation. Every time my client made any type of move in his life, he felt as if he had to worry about how it was going to affect his relationship with his friend. If he went out for a drink with someone else and didn't include this friend, he knew that this friend would hold it against him."

"Exactly what I'm talking about. What did he do?" asked Jack.

"My suggestion for him was to give his friend the Gift. The Gift is essentially the truth, the hardcore truth. You've heard the expression 'the truth hurts'—and it does in a lot of cases. The truth can also be the best cure for emotions and tensions that have been building," said Ted.

"Ted, there's no way I can come right out and tell most of these people the truth," said Jack. "I mean, I'm dealing with egos and a lot of money. Some of these situations are loaded with dynamite… like my family, my brother, my father. These require a lot of finesse."

"I know what you mean. It can be hard to confront or disappoint our own family. I learned to give the Gift many years ago, when I experienced an incident with my father that had me very uncomfortable. For a long time, I had something on my mind that I wanted to tell my father. Rather than come clean, I allowed it to eat away at me."

Ted suddenly jerked the wheel and the truck veered off the pavement to avoid a blue Studebaker that had decided to hit the brakes right in front of him.

"People!" Ted shouted, then laughed. "All this would be so easy if it weren't for employees and customers and people."

Jack joined in and they both had a good laugh. After Ted got the truck back on the road, he continued.

"Week after week, I kept taking this problem to other people, and to my own mentor and coach. Each time I kept looking for some way to work around my dad, but nothing was working and I was driving everyone, including myself, crazy."

"Oh, I've got a doozy of a problem with my own father right now," said Jack. "He started this one business, then he got sick, and my brother and I had to step in. We saved his rear end, and were glad to do it, don't get me wrong, but now he wants to sit on the sidelines and criticize and control everything, and it's become a huge roadblock and annoyance." Jack asked, "What did you do with your dad?"

"My mentor suggested I give him the Gift. The next day I sat with my father and told him what had been bugging me. I'd be lying to say it was easy, but once I got started it just all rolled out at once. The result was surprising," said Ted. "He started treating me with a sort of newfound respect. I mean, he pushed back on me for sure, and that's fine, he had his own opinion and experience.

"What was really great, though, is that we began a man-to-man discussion about reality, and with the misunderstanding cleared up, we were able to actually forge a workable solution that he would support," Ted continued. "It was a little rocky for a while but, in truth, the way forward was actually less stressful than it was to walk around on eggshells and try not to say a bunch of sarcastic stuff hoping he'd 'figure it out.'"

"Did you find a solution? Did you work it out?" asked Jack.

"Yes. We settled our differences in the weeks ahead and it wasn't long before the whole thing was forgotten," said Ted.

"Interesting," Said Jack. "I once read of a study where people were asked that if they had something in their nose, would they want the other person to tell them, and how 100% of the people said 'YES! They would want to know, and they would want the person across from them to tell them straight out."

"Well, that seems obvious," said Ted, brushing his nose involuntarily.

"Exactly. But the curious thing is, they later asked the same people what they would do if they were sitting across the table from someone with something in their nose. They went to all these ridiculous antics of brushing their nose, tapping with a finger, or a napkin, or even staring at it so the other person would figure it out without them having to say directly."

"Oh, that's human nature for you, right?" said Ted.

"Yes, that's it. Human nature," agreed Jack. "We all want the truth as clearly and as fast as we can get it, but we are conversely reluctant to tell anyone something we think they do not want to hear."

"Jack, my friend, I love that story and I'm officially stealing it to tell my coaching clients when I tell them to give the Gift. 'The Nosey Study.'"

Both men laughed easily. After some time passed, Ted spoke again.

"Giving the Gift is a lot like releasing the brakes. When you look down at your plans and strategies and tell me that there's a person standing right in the way, that's almost always a clear sign you are not telling them the truth," said Ted. "And, no matter how much we want to think we're noble or clever for not wanting to hurt someone else's feelings, we're getting harmed as much as they are.

"Take another look at one of your plans there, and when you come to the person standing in the way, think of exactly what they need to know, nothing more and nothing less. Then imagine the best case—and worst case—scenario for how things might proceed if you gave them the critical information."

Jack looked down at his notes.

"Right here." He tapped the journal with his pencil. "This one right here. If I told my problem person the truth, that would make all this tap dancing and alternate planning unnecessary."

"Great," said Ted. "Get to it then."

"Wow!" said Jack. "This would change everything."

The Titan

The street was dark and deserted when they pulled up in front of a huge skyscraper. Ted set the parking brake on the tired truck. The two men emerged into the glow of the streetlights that bathed the truck in a mellow pool of light.

"Good evening, Mr Whitman," called out the uniformed security guard at a large marble counter in the lobby.

"Hello, Arthur," replied Ted.

"The elevator operator has gone home, but I can take you up," said the guard. He met them at a bank of elevators and opened the one closest to the street with a key from a jingling loop attached to his belt. Inserting the key into the control panel of the elevator with a click, he rolled the lever to the top floor as he closed the door. With a slight bump, they began their ascent.

The three men rode skyward in that slightly awkward elevator silence. Arthur smiled and nodded at Jack. Jack returned the acknowledgement.

When they reached the top floor, Arthur opened the door to another expansive marble lobby. A huge walnut reception desk faced the elevator. Gleaming metal letters on the wall behind it spelling out Whitman Industries.

"Do you have the key to your office, Mr. Whitman?" Asked Arthur.

"Yes, yes, I'm all good Arthur, thank you," said Ted.

"Have a fine evening then, sir." Arthur disappeared behind the closing door of the elevator. Jack and Ted were left alone.

"Mr Whitman?" asked Jack.

"At your service!" Ted laughed and gave Jack's hand a firm shake.

"Follow me." Ted turned and walked briskly around the reception desk to a massive walnut door. The sound of the lock turning with Ted's key echoed sharply in the empty space. The minute the door opened, Jack's eyes grew wide, and he took a mental snapshot of the office of his dreams.

"So, this is what a man cave looks like in 1947?" Jack thought to himself. Dark wood paneling grew out of gray marble floors. Not the cheap paneling you'd find at a big box hardware story today, but amazing, custom milled, polished wood, with a texture that invited touch. Appropriately spaced across the walls were unusual and interesting paintings. The ceiling was an ornate wood paneling of a lighter color. A sprawling chandelier shined down on a serious piece of mahogany real estate… Ted's—Mr. Whitman's—desk.

Behind the desk was an expanse of floor-to-ceiling windows facing west. While on the street it was nearly dark, here on the top floor of this skyscraper the sunset was playing out its last shout of orange, pink, and scarlet miles away. The amber glow lit the room in a gilded warmth of muted color.

Ted sat down in the leather chair behind the big desk which was clean except for a telephone and a very thin stack of papers obviously arranged to get his attention.

Ted sifted through the papers, and Jack took a seat on the visitor side. When Ted looked up and relaxed back in his chair, he looked at Jack, who gave him the "what's going on here?" stare.

"Okay, I brought you here to show you the other side of what I do," said Ted.

"The other side?" asked Jack. "This is a pretty incredible other side for a guy who delivers printing all day in an old truck."

"Yes," Ted agreed, "but they really do meet in the middle."

"This I've gotta hear," said Jack.

"Well, obviously, I run a big company," Ted began. "Whitman Industries is a multi-million dollar, international conglomerate with manufacturing facilities all over the USA and Canada, and we just built our first plant in Mexico. We make everything from aircraft parts to toys and all sorts of products in between. These days I don't even know about half of the new products we're making since our plastics division started. You can make anything you can think of out of plastic, it seems."

"Impressive," said Jack, truly impressed.

"My father started this company about ten years after the Civil War ended. He was only twenty-five years old, but somehow he managed to get a government contract to supply wagons for the army right here in the Land of Lincoln, and over the years he diversified to stage coaches, and later railroad cars," said Ted. "I'm pretty proud of my father."

"Hey, I'll bet you are." Jack smiled. "I'm very proud of my father, too. He's a stubborn S.O.B and he's not perfect, but he gave me my entrepreneurial blood, and for that I'm truly grateful."

"Tell me about that stubborn part!" said Ted. "They used to say my dad was as stubborn as a government mule that just ate dinner."

Both men laughed.

"Okay, you own a giant international manufacturing company, so tell me, why you were playing hooky today instead of up here doing your job?" asked Jack, joking but firm.

"Jack, I grew up in this company. As far back as I can remember, there's been an office, and employees, and large sheds or buildings with men and women making mechanical things amidst loud noises and machinery. I started sweeping the floors in a wagon wheel manufacturing operation, and I really did work my way up the hard way.

"Now my father is gone for some years, and I'm the guy at the top. I'm not complaining about this job or this company. I'm grateful and blessed. But, Jack…," Ted leaned in across the desk and lowered his voice, "I just got bored."

"Bored?" Jack blurted out. Ted had surprised him in the middle of his success story. "You didn't have anything to do?"

"Oh, there's always plenty to do, but for me it was all easy, too much the same.

Plenty to do but no challenge," said Ted. "There comes a point in a successful company when you worry less and less about innovation and risk taking. The management gets older, people retire, and everyone starts to think a lot more about playing not to lose, rather than playing to win."

"Ah," Jack nodded. "I understand. I can see how that makes sense, too."

"Sure it does. Like I said, I'm not upset or angry about any of the evolution of this company. Why, I would be a fool to risk the jobs and security of all these people to solve my own boredom," said Ted, waving his arm at all the invisible employees.

"This is a serious business, not a toy. My father ran it that way, and I do, too."

"Are we getting to the truck driver part?" asked Jack again.

"Yes, of course. About a year ago I started to get very interested in small business startups. I began taking the odd business trip with some of our salespeople to call on people who were using our products, or selling them, at the smallest possible level. The sales people were nervous as heck at first. I mean, why was the CEO of the company riding along with them to these tiny accounts?"

"I'll bet. Go on, please. This is great!" said Jack.

"I asked a lot of questions about how they started, what their struggles were, what they learned from experience, where they thought their business was headed, and what they needed in order to get there," said Ted. "It was amazing how similar many of the challenges were to what we face here at Whitman, but how difficult they were at that level.

"Instead of satisfying my curiosity, it got me more excited and interested, mostly because of one key difference between what they were doing and what I was doing," said Ted.

"What's that?" asked Jack.

"Speed of implementation, Jack—rapid deployment of new ideas." Ted now appeared more like the energized guy who pulled him from the river than the weary CEO who plopped down in his chair to read the mail.

"These guys have things flying at them all the time, and they have to solve problems fast, and make things happen. It's the business version of what my friend Roy tells me about flying fighter planes over France in the big war!" said Ted.

"The truck?" asked Jack one more time.

"So, I took a month off from work and told everyone here I was going out of the country and not to contact me. I told them I was burned out and I'd talk to them when I came back. But, I didn't go out of town. I started a printing business!"

"You've got to be kidding me!" exclaimed Jack.

"Nope. I took a few dollars and started the business from scratch. I figured it out, put all my time into it, made sales calls, and got things going. I made the initial deliveries myself and got to know the customers. We met a couple of them today, like the pawn shop owner down on Maxwell Street.

"When I came back to work here, I started driving this truck around and delivered printing a couple of times a month. I still work in the business," he said, "and the really great part is that none of the people at the printing company know that I run this company, and no one here knows about the printing company."

"That's a really amazing story, Ted," said Jack. "In fact, it's been an amazing day for me all the way around, starting with thinking I was drowning in the Chicago River and then riding around with you, and now here."

He paused and gazed out the sheet of glass behind Ted's desk, with the city he loved in darkness. Uncountable twinkling, man-made lights transformed the landscape to magic. He had an overwhelming sense of unreality sitting in this place out of time, like waking up early in a strange hotel room and taking a moment to figure out where you are. What was happening to him?

Pulling himself back into the present, Jack asked the obvious question. "Since you are keeping your adventure in two worlds a secret from..."

"From everyone," Ted filled in the blank.

"From everyone," Jack continued, "then why have you told me, of all people? A guy you think is probably crazy, who you pulled out of the river, and who claims he's from the future?"

Ted turned his chair around and looked out at the same distant sunset. "Because you, my strange friend, are the missing piece of the puzzle."

"Me? What puzzle? What are you talking about?" asked Jack.

"All day long I've listened to you—a business owner with multiple, hot potato businesses yourself—have these conversations with all the different people in all these startup businesses. Every conversation eventually came around to what I know is your big question: Should you keep doing what you are doing, or should you sell off four of your businesses and take one as your life's work ...and drive it as big as you can get it—your own Whitman Industries—or should you jump way out on a limb, chuck the whole thing and become a business coach and mentor, and do some kind of consulting and speaking, and write a book?" Ted paused. "Is that about right?"

"Wow, said Jack, "You nailed me. But how does my dilemma become your missing piece of the puzzle? I don't get it?"

"Don't you see, Jack?" asked Ted softly. "I'm in exactly the same boat as you!"

"Ha!" laughed Jack. "Your boat is one hell of a lot bigger than mine."

"You know what I mean," said Ted. "I'm clearly not satisfied running my multiple companies at the maintenance level anymore, and I'm sorely tempted to spend all my time down at the printing company. But even that has started to become less interesting because I know how the rest of the story will go. I'll build the company, hire more people, use the resources to expand, and one of these days I'll be right back in this chair in one way or another. And what have I really done? What have I proven? And, more importantly, what have I given back?"

Jack nodded. Ted spoke in such a remarkably clear way; they thought so much alike.

"Well, Ted, what do you want to do?" he asked.

"I'm glad you asked!" Ted pulled a drawer out from the bottom of his desk and fished out a fat stack of paper. He plopped it down in front of Jack. "Here's the book I've been working on."

Jack was speechless as he pulled the bundle toward him and stared. This was surely the most industrious man he had ever met. He was running a multi-million dollar company in post World War II without any of the digital technology that Jack had at his disposal to run a speck of businesses by comparison, living a second-life job as a startup printing company owner, and personally delivering the product… and he found time in there somewhere to write what appeared to be a four-hundred page book on business—on a typewriter, no less!

"What the heck is this, Ted?" he asked.

It's Not the Economy, It's the People

"I know a little diner that serves a great supper back toward the lake," said Ted, shifting gears and easing the truck onto the nearly empty street.

"I'm starved," said Jack. When was the last time he'd had food? Was the donut really his last meal?

He pulled out the journal Ted had given him and made some more notes. The conversation with Ted in the office had been very enlightening. He was starting to connect the dots. Jack smiled at the title he had given his notes.

Jack tucked the leather journal into the pocket of his jacket, reached over to the fat stack of papers on the bench seat between them, and plopped Ted's book draft in his lap. Flipping through the pages, he scanned and read chapter titles and sections of text that caught his eye.

"Wow, Ted," he said, "you've really done some hard work here."

"Thanks Jack," said Ted, smiling.

"I expected this to be really wordy but I like how you've boiled down years of your experience into these simple principles," said Jack.

"Did you notice the case studies?" asked Ted.

"Yes! I love case studies. When you put yourself in another business owner's shoes and see how problems and challenges develop, you can learn so much," Jack replied. "I mean, it's like these people are taking all the risks and trying things, and I can see what worked for them. I can also see some red flags I wouldn't have seen before."

"These case studies are timeless in my opinion," said Ted. "I mean, some of them are from more than ten years ago, but even though we have all these fancy electronic gadgets now, and business has really changed from 1937 to now, one thing stays the same."

"What's that?" asked Jack.

"People," said Ted. "No matter what direction the challenges come from, inside the business or outside, it's almost always a people problem."

"A people problem," Jack repeated. "How do you mean?"

"Dealing with people takes the most time," said Ted. "It's the most complicated and requires the most skill. All the things we do in business, I believe, really boil down to choosing people who have solid values, developing clear communication, and setting boundaries and expectations. You can't just push people in a box and expect them to perform like a machine. You have to have a ton of patience."

Jack thought about his business. Ted was right. It was all about people. His partners, his customers, his vendors, his family and friends were the reality behind the paper and money that measured his business. He smiled. His love for building businesses was really his love for people.

Ted continued. "I started out taking notes about the businesses I visited with the salespeople. Then it grew, and I started sorting things out by category. It just kept growing with the startup of the printing company. Calling on these different businesses, delivering the printing has turned into multiple case studies, and now I have this leviathan, this monster, and it's all real," said Ted patting the loose pages of his book.

"This is just amazing," said Jack. "I know I am saying 'amazing' a lot Ted, but this is..."

"It's a lot of business wisdom, collected from real businesses. Dozens of startup companies as seen through the eyes of someone who's built one of the largest companies in America," said Ted.

Ted was looking straight ahead paying close attention to the road. Jack looked closely at Ted's face as they went in and out of pools of light created by the occasional street light or traffic light. The man was without a hint of ego.

Amazing!

In the darkness, the truth dawned on Jack. "You want to publish this as a book, and go full time helping other business people, don't you?" he said.

"Yes, Jack ...all day long as you've been talking about what you should do. I hope that's clearer for you now and if it is, I'm really glad," said Ted. "What you do is for you to decide. I can't tell you what is right for you, but I think you know. I now know for sure what's right for me, and I have you and your crazy time travel story and spending the day with you to thank."

Ted paused, and after a few seconds Jack nearly shouted, "Well, what?"

"I'm selling this company, keeping the printing company as an experiment, publishing this book, and spending the rest of my life funding and advising startup-minded entrepreneurs," said Ted.

They hit a pothole in the road with a solid thud, the truck shuddered and bounced back on its springs.

"Didn't see that one," said Ted. "You okay?"

When Jack did not reply Ted glanced over to the passenger side of the truck, but it was empty.

Jack was gone.

Back to the Future

Sirens wailed, voices shouted, sounds of machinery and motors rattled loudly, and the air smelled of gasoline and burning rubber. Jack opened his eyes and saw nothing but the Chicago River through the broken glass of what used to be his windshield.

His hands went reflexively to his face and, sure enough, that wetness he felt was blood. On full reflex mode now, he lowered his hands into view and looked at his own blood smeared on his hands. His heart raced.

"Don't move!" a woman's voice shouted in his ear, startling him and making him jump. She sounded as if she was just inches from his ear. Jack turned to his left, and there was a short, red-haired, female police officer apparently standing on the running board of his SUV. Her eyes were wide and she seemed to be leaning at a strange angle.

"What?" asked Jack, dazed.

"Do not move, sir!" she barked again, too loudly. "Look! You're hanging on the edge of this bridge, and if you start moving around you may go right off into the water. So don't move until we get a cable on you."

Jack looked around and realized his vehicle was dangling over the edge of the bridge, tilting down to the water. The seat belt pinched his chest tightly, and now he knew why. It was keeping him from falling through the windshield into the water!

The police woman shouted toward the back of the truck, "Yes! Ok. Go, go, go!"

He felt a sharp jolt pulling the vehicle backward, and the seat belt dug deeper into his chest, forcing the air out of his lungs. The SUV squealed loudly as the cable from the tow truck hauled it back to the street above, scraping the concrete bridge walls which tumbled down into the river. Slowly he came back to a normal, vertical seated position.

"Good. That's good." The police woman waved back toward the back again, and the movement of the vehicle stopped. "Get him outta there!" she shouted, and a group of paramedics and fire fighters descended on Jack, rapidly but gently extricating him from the bent metal and glass.

They flatboarded him out of the vehicle and onto a waiting stretcher. As the paramedics lifted him up into the ambulance, he overheard someone whispering behind him, "Can you believe that? He should have totally gone into the river."

"I know!" said a second voice that sounded like the police woman. "When I came up to him he was totally unconscious. With that cut on his head and bleeding like that, if he'd gone swimming I think he'd have drowned."

Jack felt the stretcher bed being locked in place, and watched as a paramedic jumped in from the back and took a seat next to him. Smiling, he said, "Hello! What's your name?" He began to tear open sterile packages and clean Jack's bloody face.

"Jack. I'm Jack." he said, eyes clenched as the paramedic continued to wash his face.

"Well, today you get a new name," said the paramedic.

"What?" asked Jack.

"Your new name is One Lucky S.O.B.!" He laughed and patted Jack's shoulder.

The ambulance began to move away slowly, but suddenly someone was banging hard on the back double doors. The paramedic peeked out, nodded his head, and opened the door. It was the red-headed police woman. She had something in her hand. She lifted it up where he could see from his lying down position and asked, "You need this?"

It was the leather journal Ted had given him.

"Yes, he nodded." She pressed it into his outstretched palm and smiled. "Good luck, sir. You'll be fine."

Overwhelmed by the shock, the relief, and the pain that was starting to throb in his head, Jack pulled the journal to his chest, struggling to fight back tears. One Lucky S.O.B. indeed. He smiled at the paramedic's joke. Taking a long, deep breath, he sighed and closed his eyes. The paramedic injected something into his arm, and Jack felt a heavy wave of sleepiness wash over him as the pain faded. He closed his eyes.

Upon Reflection

"There!" said Jack. "Right there." He was pointing to a section of the bridge across the intersection. Instead of the old, grainy concrete, the cement on this section was smooth and new.

"Let's park just up ahead. I want to walk back to this exact spot," Jack said to his twenty-four-year old son.

"If you say so, Dad," said his son with more than a hint of sarcasm. "I think that bump on your head gave you the whole time travel thing."

"Jordy, we've been over this," said Jack. "I can't explain it, but I can't shake it either. I think it will be helpful to put my feet right on the spot where it happened. Maybe then I can put it away."

"Well, the whole time travel thing aside, I actually think it's a great idea for you to go back to where you had such a smash fest. I think it would freak most people out," said Jordan. "I'm proud of you, Dad."

Jack nodded agreement to his son. Jordan knew he was just as proud of him. They parked, and Jack quickly jumped out of the vehicle. He walked briskly toward the bridge. He was staring down at the water when his son walked up and stood beside him.

"For a guy with his leg in a cast, you sure can motor!" said Jordan, laughing.

Jack did not reply, but nodded. He was having a very strange sensation standing at the exact spot where he had plunged off the bridge.

"Wow!" said Jordan. "That must have been a ride." Jack agreed as they both surveyed the distance from where they stood to the river. The occasional Sunday driver went by unnoticed by the pair. They were silent for a long time.

"Jordy, I went down there," said Jack.

"I know you did, Dad." Jordan patted his Dad's solid arm as Jack gripped the railing a little too tightly. His Dad was a guy's guy who'd taught him to box, and still played street hockey at an age when most guys didn't exercise at all. He was not used to seeing his father rattled.

"You went down there, all right. You were hit hard and you slammed into the water," Jordan continued softly, "and when the cops and the paramedics got here, you came right back out and into an ambulance to the hospital."

"Hey!" said Jack. "They say you never believe in ghosts—until you see one. Something happened to me that's so far beyond a dream or hallucination. I gotta track this thing down."

"Alright, Dad," said Jordan. "I signed up for this crazy tour, so let's get going."

Jack patted his son's shoulder, and they headed back to the car. Jack opened up the leather journal he'd been carrying around since the accident. He had drawn a map of his adventure from memory.

"Go up here and make a U-turn," he said. "Ted took me that way into the city."

The rest of the day they hunted down buildings and places he'd seen with Ted.

Flo's Coffee Shop was now a convenience store. The high ceiling and light fixtures were the same though. He'd been there. The Whitman Industries Building was still there, an impressive skyscraper that reached to the sky. The cornerstone identified it as being built by Ted Whitman, though the steel and glass sign announced it was now owned by a wi-fi company.

Jordan watched as his father scribbled notes and bounced his attention between the places they were visiting and the notes he was taking.

"Well, Dad, we've checked 'em all off, right?" said Jordan. "Ready to head home?"

"Not yet, son," said Jack. "I've saved the best for last. Get on the freeway up here and head east."

"Where we going?" asked Jordan.

"Maxwell Street, son," Jack answered.

On the way, Jack regaled his son with tales of Maxwell Street legend and history. He told him about his own roots, and stories about his uncles and grandparents, many of whose names Jordan had only vaguely heard.

They parked and walked down into the historic part of Maxwell Street. Though much had changed, Jack was able to point out many of the locations, and anchored the stories he had been telling his son to real physical places.

The two men, deep in conversation and immersed in thoughts, stopped at a café and sat down. The waitress took their order for coffee. They sat outside in front of the cafe as an eclectic parade of people walked by. Ethnic music rose and fell, and dozens of sounds, conversations and laughter filled the air.

"Well, Dad, now that you've been to all these places, how are you feeling?" asked Jordan.

"Good, son," said Jack with a smile, stirring the coffee that had just arrived. "And I've got a couple of important things I want to share with you."

"Sure, Dad," said Jordan. "What've you got? You gonna tell me you were abducted by aliens, too?"

They laughed.

"Okay, first, I'm going to write a book," he said. He'd never told anyone what he'd been thinking, and it felt good to announce it first to his son.

"A book, huh?" said Jordan. "What about?"

"I want to expand the ideas I got from that day, son," said Jack. "I've spent my whole life kicking butt in business… driving, pushing, and always hustling for success in whatever I've done."

"So, a book about success?" asked Jordan.

"Well, not exactly," said Jack, "at least not in the ordinary way. I believe that for people who've paid the price and become successful, there's a new question they come to about what to do next."

"How do you mean?" asked Jordan.

"Some people who've made a lot of money, or pushed a business to the top, reach the point where they're no longer focused so much on growing the business, but more on managing, playing not to lose—or they're just buried alive in details and management, and they're not happy doing it," said Jack.

"Okay, I see what you mean," replied Jordan. He paused. "How do you know this?"

"Well, for some reason these people seem to seek me out," said Jack. "I meet people all the time that you and I would think are very successful, but when you get inside their head they are frustrated, stressed out, and sometimes burned out.

"When they lose the fire that drove them to the top, they start thinking about all sorts of options. Some of them want to bail, walk away, or do something really radical that they've never done before."

"So, that sounds like a problem," said Jordan. "Would your book be one of your famous kick-butt pep talks? You gonna tell 'em to get motivated and get back to work?"

"Not exactly, son," said Jack. "They may need to do that, but not until they're certain they are putting their energy into the right way forward. Look at this..."

Jack wheeled around the leather journal to the center of the table so that his son could read it. Jordan looked at the handful of lines:

The Titan Principles:

- Know Your Story
- Draw the Line
- Never Be Satisfied
- Give the Gift
- People – People - People

"I've heard you talk about all of these things, Dad," said Jordan, "Good stuff, I know."

"Thanks, Jordy. What I learned in what you call 'the time travel thing' was how they all work together to create a special kind of filter. You see, people who are facing the challenge of what to do after being successful—where do I go from here?—is that there is so much clutter and confusion in the way, they can't really see their options clearly.

"In the book, I want to take them through a quick burst of challenges to help them clear up this confusion, so they can make a good reliable choice. It goes like this:

"Number One – Know Your Story… your past, your traits, your heritage—all of the things that brought you here. When you clearly see the markers in your life and business you can see where you are on the bigger map of your life, and where to go next.

"Once they do the exercises I'll put in the book, I think they'll have a big wakeup call - a big A-HA about so many things. When they do this I think about half of the confusion will just disappear.

"Number Two – Draw the Line. Once you eliminate the things that aren't really right for you, you take the choices and actions you have left, put them on a worksheet, and decide what it would take to make them happen.

"This step is about getting real and honest… cutting out the whining and mystery we all trash up our thinking with.

"Dad, this is really good," said Jordan, demonstrating some uncharacteristic enthusiasm for his Dad's philosophies. "You already got me thinking about some choices I have about my own future. Go on!"

Jack was in a zone now. He continued.

"Number Three – Never Be Satisfied. The reason this is important, and the reason it is in this spot, is that the minute you really do the Draw the Line work, it is very natural to get discouraged or overwhelmed by the challenges and the blowback you are going to get from other people.

"Now is the time you need to apply that kick butt motivation you talked about. This is when, in order to do extraordinary things, or to even do the right things, you need to get a quick antidote to complacency. Never Be Satisfied is not about being a demanding jerk," said Jack.

They both laughed.

"We don't know anyone like that, do we, Dad?" joked Jordan.

"Easy, sport!" Jack acknowledged his son's joke with a smile.

"Never Be Satisfied is really about taming that doubt we all have. Instead of looking for an easy way out, we imagine something that will be challenging. But it is in solving those challenges that we are truly inspired not just to do big things, but to do the things that are right for us." Jack tapped the journal with his finger loudly for emphasis.

"Number Four – People - People - People… because entrepreneurs often get so caught up in their own heads about money, finance, success, sales, products, meetings, blah, blah, blah," said Jack with mock annoyance. "We get so up in our heads about the business, thinking we have to be smarter than everyone, that we become control freaks …and we isolate ourselves.

"We get into this egotistical, stressed-out thinking that leads us to think that we have no reliable help. What I want people see is that when you shift your focus to helping develop the people God has put in your life, then you get two big benefits.

"One, you get a whole team of brains solving problems and watching your back, and their strength will carry you to bigger success than you could ever achieve alone.

"Two, you end up with a life of meaning as you filter the love and passion you have for your business and values through the real lives of people. When you realize that all the money in the world won't make you happy, or keep you alive for another two hundred years, your life will be rich beyond compare, and a lot more fun… if you remember it's all about the people."

"Wow, Dad. I'm impressed," said Jordan, looking down at the journal. He was looking inside his own heart.

"Finally, Number Five – Give the Gift. No matter how brave or outspoken or how honest we are, we all struggle with telling people things they don't want to hear. In the life of an entrepreneur there is almost always resistance."

"And that resistance usually comes in the form of those same people you were just talking about, right?" asked Jordan.

Jack, stopped short. His son was right on the beam. He smiled. "Exactly, Jordy. I couldn't have said it better myself. In fact, I'm stealing that sentence for the book!

"Yes. We dance around, telling people what they don't want to hear because of fear. When we reach the point where we're ready to move forward it's vital that we clear up this resistance, deal with this fear, get the truth on the table, and tell that person the real hard truth.

"I call it Giving the Gift, because in reality we all want to know the truth even if it's hard to hear, inconvenient, or expensive and costs us something at first. In our position as business owners or leaders, it's vital that we get people to be honest with us, and we must teach by example and give that gift to others.

"If we go through these steps, we get an amazing clarity about dealing with that confusion, the stress of choices, or burnout, and we can move forward with power and clarity."

The two men sipped their coffee in silence, both lost in their thoughts. Finally, Jack spoke up and asked, "Well, what do you think, son?"

"What are you going to call it?" he asked.

"The Titan," said Jack.

"Dad, seriously, I think it sounds like a great book, and I think it could help a lot of people," he said. "I just have one suggestion."

"Tell me," said Jack.

"Just don't make it based on your crazy time travel hallucination!"

They both laughed, but Jordan caught a twinkle in his Dad's eye and a mischievous smile. That was exactly what the old man was going to do. And, in his own way, he knew his father had just given him "The Gift" of truth.

"Okay, you said you had a couple of things you want to share with me. A book is huge, but what is the other thing?" asked Jordan.

"Come on." Jack tossed some cash on the table for the coffee and a tip, and stood up.

They walked to the street, looked both ways instinctively, and crossed over.

Jack pointed to the cluttered window of what must have been a pawn shop for decades. "Well, what do you think?"

"Think about what?" asked Jordan, eyeing the shop window with curiosity.

"I bought this place." Jack announced proudly.

"WHAT? You have got to be joking?" shouted Jordan.

"Nope, it's a done deal," said Jack, reaching for the door.

They walked through the door into a high-ceiled, historic building. At the back was a gigantic, saloon-style bar that served as the sales counter. The building was stuffed with everything from tools to antiques.

Jordan was wide-eyed and silent, trying to take it in. "What in the world are you going to do with this place, Dad?" he asked quietly.

"I think you are gonna find the history of this place very interesting, son. The warehouse for this place is as big as an airplane hangar and stuffed with antiques that the owner had no idea were more than junk," said Jack.

"Seriously?" asked Jordan, wheels spinning.

"I wonder if maybe you have some ideas on how to grow this business with me...and maybe," Jack asked quietly, "you'd even want to be a part of it, son?"

What's Next?

Got questions?

What happened next?

Did Ted write his book?

Want to find out more?

FREE STUFF!

Go to www.LiveToWinCoaching.com now to get instant access to The Titan Success System and cool insider information about the real Maxwell Street story, and answers to the mysterious mentor Ted!

For personal coaching and consulting with Steve Werner, or to have Steve speak at your next meeting:

http://LiveToWinCoaching.com

Acknowledgements:

Big thanks go out to my friends and family, without whom The Titan would not have been possible.

- To my wife Jill and children Allie, Dylan, and Brett for understanding my relentless approach to success.

- To my parents and family members who helped to shape me into the person I am.

- To my business partners who allow me the flexibility to do what I love.

- To my coaches, past and present for helping me become the student and coach that I have become.

- To Rick Butts for identifying early on that there was an amazing tale to tell and for his creativity in bringing it to life.

- To my brother who helped me realize that age and success do not always run parallel.

- And to Fr. Frank Cimmarusti who helped me believe in me... And for teaching me to "give the gift."

Steve Werner - Chicago Il - Winter 2012

About the Authors

Steve Werner

Steve Werner is an author, speaker, consultant, with an extensive background in starting and building entrepreneurial businesses. A lifetime entrepreneur, many of the stories in The Titan, like selling watches at the open air market in Phoenix out of his 1977 Trans Am are based on his own real life experiences.

A graduate of Arizona State University, Werner became an Independent Floor Trader (30 Yr Treasury Bonds) at The Chicago Board of Trade for 19 years, then began reorganized and partnering in one of Chicago's largest private real estate lending operations designed for rehabbers and investors He is currently a partner in a private real estate lending and development company and a partner in a company that secures vacant property in the Chicago area.

Steve is married to Jill for 23 years and has three great children, Allie 22, Dylan 20, and Brett 16, in Chicago Illinois.

Steve is an executive and CEO level coach and consultant, who specializes in helping top performers to redirect their careers after success, turning the "what do I do now?" into purpose, passion, and intentional success!

www.LiveToWinCoaching.com

Rick Butts

Rick Butts is an author of 14 books, and a recovering motivational speaker.

Touring rock musician/singer until age 30, Rick traded his guitar for a suit and tie, building business startups until discovering his passion to speak and write, traveling internationally for a decade as a keynote speaker for top corporations and associations.

He is an expert helping idea people monetize their creativity and has created multiple programs available online at RickButts.com.

Rick splits his time living in the Rocky Mountains of Denver Colorado, and Odessa Ukraine on the Black Sea.

http://RickButts.com

Made in the USA
Lexington, KY
29 October 2013